KU-766-373

To the reader:

Welcome to the DK ELT Graded Readers! These readers are different. They explore aspects of the world around us: its history, geography, science ... and a lot of other things. And they show the different ways in which people live now, and lived in the past.

These DK ELT Graded Readers give you material for reading for information, and reading for pleasure. You are using your English to do something real. The illustrations will help you understand the text, and also help bring the Reader to life. There is a glossary to help you understand the special words for this topic. Listen to the cassette or CD as well, and you can really enter the world of the Olympic Games, the *Titanic*, or the Trojan War ... and a lot more. Choose the topics that interest you, improve your English, and learn something ... all at the same time.
Enjoy the series!

To the teacher:

This series provides varied reading practice at five levels of language difficulty, from elementary to FCE level:
BEGINNER
ELEMENTARY A
ELEMENTARY B
INTERMEDIATE
UPPER INTERMEDIATE
The language syllabus has been designed to suit the factual nature of the series, and includes a wider vocabulary range than is usual with ELT readers: language linked with the specific theme of each book is included and glossed. The language scheme, and ideas for exploiting the material (including the recorded material) both in and out of class are contained in the Teacher's Resource Book.
We hope you and your students enjoy using this series.

Dorling Kindersley

LONDON, NEW YORK, SYDNEY, DELHI,
PARIS, MUNICH & JOHANNESBURG

Originally published as Eyewitness Reader
Extreme Machines in 2000 and adapted as an
ELT Graded Reader for
Dorling Kindersley by

studio cactus ©

13 SOUTHGATE STREET WINCHESTER HAMPSHIRE SO23 9DZ

Published in Great Britain by
Dorling Kindersley Limited
9 Henrietta Street, London WC2E 8PS

2 4 6 8 10 9 7 5 3 1

Copyright © 2000
Dorling Kindersley Limited, London

A CIP catalogue record for this book is
available from the British Library.

ISBN 0-7513-2927-4

Colour reproduction by Colourscan, Singapore
Printed and bound in China by
L. Rex Printing Co., Ltd
Text film output by Mick Hodson Associates, UK

The publisher would like to thank the following
for their kind permission to reproduce their photographs:
c=centre; t=top; b=below; l=left; r=right

See our complete catalogue at

www.dk.com

Contents

ELT Graded Readers

ELEMENTARY B

MOVING MACHINES

Written by Susan Woolard

Series Editor Susan Holden

A Dorling Kindersley Book

On land

In 1993, the *Endeavor* became the fastest truck in the world. It travelled at an amazing 363 kph, and broke the world land speed record.

On the sea

Offshore powerboats can travel on the sea more than three times faster than a car can travel on the motorway.

An Extreme Machine

Most of the cars, boats, and planes we travel in today are very safe and work well. We see them every day in our towns and cities, and they don't surprise us. They are a normal part of everyday life. But there are many other machines that can surprise us! These strange-looking machines are not for people to travel in. They are made to do something amazing – for example they go very fast or they fly really high.

These are extreme machines – this means they are the fastest/biggest/highest machines of their kind in the world. Extreme machines are amazing; most people are interested in seeing them, and would like to get close to them. Some people would like to do even better – they'd like to ride in them!

In this book you will learn more about some of the strangest machines in the world – what they look like and what they can do. You will also learn a little about how they work. We will look at the people who put their own lives in danger to ride the extreme machines.

In the air
The space shuttle is built to make many trips into space, and it is big enough to carry a lot of things inside. In fact, it could even carry a small whale!

Ray power
Solar cars use the power of the sun's rays, not petrol or diesel. This car, called the *Mad Dog*, can achieve speeds of more than 70 kph (but not on cloudy days!).

5

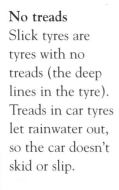

Drag Car Racing

Two drivers were sitting in their drag cars, waiting for the next 400-metre race. They watched as someone put water over all the tyres (or slicks) at the back of the cars. This made the fat slicks smoother and easier to slip. Each driver put one foot down hard on the front brakes and with the other foot he pressed the accelerator.

The noise from the car engines was very loud, and everyone in the crowd shouted and cheered. The cars were not moving forwards, but the slicks started turning round and round. Everyone could see smoke – it was rising up behind the slicks.

No treads
Slick tyres are tyres with no treads (the deep lines in the tyre). Treads in car tyres let rainwater out, so the car doesn't skid or slip.

After a few seconds, the slicks on the cars got hotter and hotter, and they became softer. Now they were not so dangerous, and they could hold on to the ground very well when they were travelling. The wheels wouldn't slip – even when the drivers suddenly started to move very fast.

Each driver now put his car into first gear. The engine was very loud, and he had to hold tightly on to the handbrake to stop the car moving. Then the drivers could feel their cars pulling forwards, and it was difficult to hold on to the brakes. Waiting like this was the worst part of the race, and made everyone feel excited and nervous.

In front of the drivers were a lot of lights, one on top of the other – they looked like a Christmas tree. All eyes were on the "tree". The drivers were looking hard at the lights, ready to move as soon as they changed colour.

Best ever
The fastest recorded drag car took only 5.63 seconds to travel over 400 metres. That is six times faster than a racehorse.

Slow car?
A Ferrari can get from 0 to 100 kph in about five seconds. Drag racers do this in two seconds!

First one of the lights came on, and then another. Then a green light came on, and the two cars jumped forwards very fast.

This kind of racing is very different from races like Le Mans or Formula One. There are only two cars, but you have to watch very carefully at a drag car race – if you close your eyes for a moment you could miss the race! Less than eight seconds later, the cars went across the finish line – this was 400 metres down the track. In this time, the cars got up to 240 kph – that is twice as fast as a car on a motorway.

Drag racers often have a parachute to help them stop. This is kept in a small box behind the driver's seat.

Because the drag cars were travelling so fast, it was very difficult to stop. So the drivers used parachutes to help them to slow down. The parachutes were like strong brakes, pushing against the air and pulling the car back.

The two cars finished very close together this time, and it was hard for the excited people in the crowd to see which car won. Luckily, the organisers could use an electronic timer to check the times and decide the winner. This time, the winner was the driver of the car on the left, but he was only seven-hundredths of a second faster than the other car!

After the race was finished, the loser drove off the track and the winner drove back along a special road to start his next race. Both drivers got a small piece of paper that told them their time for the race, and their speed at the end.

The winning driver had a very good day. He had seven races in two hours, and he won all of them. But the amazing thing is that because each race is very short, in all that time he was racing for less than a minute!

Not so fast
A drag bike is slower than a drag car. This is because it can easily go up on its back wheel if it goes too fast. This would make the bike travel even more slowly.

Slower again
Drag trucks are slower than drag cars and drag bikes, because they are bigger and heavier. It takes them twice as long as drag cars to travel the 400 metres of the special race track.

At Le Mans, cars go round a circuit (a racetrack that starts and finishes in the same place, like a circle) that is about twelve kilometres long. They go round this circuit about 350 times in the race.

Running start
In the past, drivers started the Le Mans race outside their cars – they ran across the track and jumped into them. But this was dangerous and it doesn't happen now.

Le Mans

One of the most famous and difficult car races in the world is at a track near Le Mans (a town in France). Every year, in May and June, the town of Le Mans is very busy and full of people. All the big racing cars are there, with their drivers and special teams of workers. And because this race is very famous, thousands of people come to watch.

The cars have come there to be in a long, hard 24-hour race around the circuit near the town. It is very fast, it is very tiring, and, of course, for many people it is very exciting. The winners will have their photographs in newspapers around the world.

On the day of the race, there are between seventy and eighty cars at the starting line. It is an amazing thing to see! Then the race starts, and the cars travel round and round the circuit all day – and it takes only a few minutes to do one circuit.

The circuit at Le Mans is only twelve kilometres long. This does not seem like a long way, but when they get to the end of the race, cars have travelled nearly 4,888 kilometres. This is the same as travelling across the USA, then coming more than a third of the way back!

It is very difficult for one driver to do this race alone, so each car has a team of three drivers. The drivers in the team change places after fifteen circuits. This means that each person drives for about one hour and then stops for a rest.

It is very important for the drivers to stay awake, because if they get tired in a race like this, it is very easy to crash. When a car crashes, the organisers have to get it off the track as soon as possible before more cars crash into it. Usually, if a car breaks down on the road, someone will pull it away – this is called a tow. All cars at Le Mans must have a special towing eye at the front and back, and this makes it easier to tow the car off the track quickly. You can see the towing eye at the front of car number five in the picture here.

Wet or dry?
Tyres with lines cut in them (the tread) are used when it rains. Smooth, flat tyres with no tread are used when it's dry.

Used once
Windscreens get damaged easily in the race, so they are used only once.

Low = fast
Le Mans cars are very low – about one metre high – and very wide. This helps them to hold the track and stay on the ground at high speed.

Quick change
It is important to change tyres very quickly in a race. Usually a car wheel has four nuts that hold it on to the car – but a racing car wheel has only one nut so it is faster to get it off and on.

Who's that?
Racing cars have big numbers on the top and sides. It is easy to see the numbers, even when the cars are going very fast.

The best place to watch the race at Le Mans is somewhere near the pits. The pits are special areas where mechanics change the tyres, add petrol, and fix any problems with the car or the engine. Cars often drive into the pits during the race, looking for more petrol or new tyres. So if you stand near there, you will see all the drivers at some time coming in to stop. It is easier than trying to see them racing past on their circuit!

As soon as a car comes into the pits, the mechanics in the team are all over it – like insects. Each mechanic does one special job, and they practise this again and again until they can do it very fast. With good mechanics, the car gets new tyres and is filled with petrol in only a few seconds. Then the driver is off again and back into the race – he doesn't want another driver to overtake him.

AVANTI 3

Strong truck
This truck was in a long, difficult race called the Baja 1,000. This race is in Mexico, and it is for 1,000 kilometres – but not on roads. The race is over rocky and sandy ground.

The pits are very busy places. There are cars, with the drivers inside wanting to hurry up and get back into the race. There are the other drivers in the team, resting and waiting to change places, and of course the mechanics, working and checking everything. There are also photographers and newspaper reporters, taking pictures and writing stories about the race. Behind the pits, each team has a big garage where they keep the parts for their cars.

After visiting the pits and changing tyres, the driver has to be very careful. Cold tyres do not hold on to the ground as well as hot tyres, so they are more dangerous. It is easier to skid (slip) with cold tyres, especially if it is a fast start. This is a good test of the driver's skills. Many drivers make mistakes, and so a lot of cars never finish the race.

Engine power
The engines in Le Mans cars are very powerful – four times more powerful than in normal cars! Most engines are at the back, behind the driver, and not in the front, like family cars today.

Thrust SSC

The *Thrust* SSC (SSC means supersonic car) was designed like this for a very special reason – it was built to be the fastest car in the world, and break the world land speed record. It was also the first car to travel at supersonic speed (in other words, to go faster than the speed of sound, which is about 1,224 kph). But the team of people who built the car had big problems at first when they tried to race it. In fact, they almost stopped trying.

The team built the car in Britain, where they lived. But unfortunately they couldn't race the car there. They needed a very long, flat piece of ground to try out the car. Without this, they couldn't get it up to its top speed, and break the record. But there was nowhere like this in Britain – everywhere they looked was too short, or had hills.

Fast truck
Thrust SSC is made to move through the air as quickly as possible. It is long and thin, and holds the ground well. Its special design is aerodynamic, and this helps it to travel much faster.

However, they did know where to find a good place to race their car – Black Rock Desert, in Nevada, USA. The desert in Nevada was long, and it was very, very flat. There were no hills to slow down the car. But the Nevada Desert was very far away, and the big problem was money. The team didn't have enough money to fly their supersonic car from Britain to the USA.

Then one of the team had a good idea – they could ask other people to give them money. So they put information about the car and about their problem on the internet and in the newspapers. They asked people to buy a small amount of aeroplane fuel each (114 litres). Then the people could feel that they were helping to break a world record.

A lot of people like fast cars, and so this idea was very popular. Many people started to send in their money to buy fuel. Soon the team had all the money they wanted. They were ready to go to the USA and try to make a new world record.

Slow start
The first land speed record was made in 1898 by Gaston de Chasseloup. His final speed was 63 kph. Today, a bicycle racer could go faster than this!

Old record
The fastest car before *Thrust SSC* was called *Thrust 2*. In 1983, *Thrust 2* travelled at 1,018 kph.

A fast truck?
The *Endeavor* holds the land speed record for trucks, but *Thrust SSC* is more than three times faster than this!

A fast car?
The *Maclaren F1* is the fastest car you can drive on the street – it can travel at 370 kph. But the *Thrust SSC* can travel three times faster.

October 15th, 1997 was a beautiful autumn day. The weather was great – perfect for driving fast and trying to make a new speed record. Andy Green, the driver, sat in the seat of the *Thrust SSC*. He checked everything carefully, then slowly started to accelerate. The huge black car began to move forwards.

It moved slowly and carefully at first – it was important not to take in any of the dust of the desert as this could damage the engines. But soon Andy was driving faster and faster, and you could see flames (long lines of fire) coming out of the back. These were the afterburners working in the car's jet engines. The bright flames behind the car were twelve metres long. Everyone watching was amazed.

The driver was sitting very low down in the car, and it was difficult to see much from there. The desert was very flat, and the people standing there could see a long way, but the driver could only see three kilometres in front of him. To help him to go in a straight line (the fastest way), the other people in the team made a white line along the desert floor. They used a special white powder called gypsum.

The white line helped the driver to go straight, and it also helped the team to measure the speed. There was another mark halfway along the line, and this was exactly 1.6 kilometres away. When the car got to the halfway point that day it was travelling at an amazing 1,228 kph. That is a little bit faster than the speed of sound. The car took less than five seconds to travel the 1.6 kilometres.

Everyone watched as the huge 10-tonne jet car went past. It was travelling in a straight line very smoothly, and people thought it looked like a train on rails. But behind the car, there was a huge carpet of desert dust, ninety metres wide. The shock wave behind the car lifted up the dust on the surface of the desert. A few seconds later, there were two loud bangs – this was the noise of the *Thrust*'s jet engines going faster than the speed of sound, or breaking the sound barrier.

Only two minutes after it started, the car stopped – it was now twenty kilometres from where it started. The driver and all the other people in the team were delighted – *Thrust* SSC was now officially the fastest car in the world. They had broken the world land speed record.

A fast plane?
Flying over the Nevada Desert in October 1997, you could look out of the window and get a big surprise – *Thrust* SSC moved 290 kph faster than a 747 jet aeroplane.

Getting faster
Thrust SSC broke the sound barrier on the ground exactly fifty years after the first plane (the X-1) did this in the air.

What about people?
The fastest person in the world can run 100 metres in just under ten seconds. That is about 38 kph.

Stretch Limousine

When one lucky man won a lot of money, he didn't think about it very long – he knew exactly what he wanted to do. He bought his favourite car – a Cadillac. Then he told his friends that he was going to cut the car in half. Of course, his friends thought he was crazy! But the man wanted a very special kind of car – a stretch limousine (or "limo" for short) – and to make this, you first have to cut a car in two.

He sent his car to a special factory where they made stretch limousines, and he asked for a "120-inch super stretch limo". This meant that the factory would open up the car and make the middle part (the body) longer by 120 inches (3 metres).

The factory workers cut the car in half very easily – like a knife cutting through butter. They had to put long steel rails in the middle to make a strong floor, and then they put new sides on the middle part of the car. Finally, they changed the seats and the design on the inside of the new car.

Think small
The smallest car in the world is the same size as the end of a match. The car really works, and it is a true model of a 1936 Toyota. But it is 1,000 times smaller!

Think bigger
One of the smallest cars on the road is the Smart, made by Daimler Benz. You can fit two into a parking space.

They put in a special window behind the driver's seat, and this was like a wall between the driver and the passengers. The chauffeur (driver) couldn't hear the passengers talking in the back.

They also put in electric windows, which moved up and down silently, and big, soft leather seats – very comfortable! Now it was possible for up to ten people to sit in the car. But it wasn't like sitting in a normal car – inside the stretch limo there was a refrigerator, a telephone, a television, and a video. It was like a beautiful, comfortable home (or an expensive yacht), but this home was on wheels.

All dressed up
Limousines usually have a special design inside. They may have neon lights and painted ceilings, for example. This makes them look expensive and very glamorous.

How long?
You could park six big family cars along the side of the world's longest stretch limousine.

Deep-sea Submersible

One day, two scientists and a pilot climbed inside *Alvin* a new deep-sea submersible. The *Alvin* was sitting on top of a bigger ship, and now it was ready to go into the sea. A huge crane picked up the little ship, with the two men inside, and put it down carefully on the water.

Getting dark
There is no light when you are fifty metres below sea level, and so submersibles must have very strong lights if they are going deeper.

The crane has moved the submersible from the big ship into the water.

Going down
Scuba divers can dive up to fifty metres before they have to stop, because of the water pressure. But a diver wearing a special diving suit can go ten times deeper.

The *Alvin* was seven metres long, and it sat on top of the water for a few seconds – then it dived down under the sea. Now it moved very smoothly, and as it went deeper, it looked more like a spaceship than a normal ship.

The submersible was now going down very far, almost four kilometres into the black water of the deep ocean. The journey took a little more than two hours.

The crew (the men working inside the ship) were wearing special thermal underwear and big sweaters to keep them warm. The water outside was icy cold and it was difficult to keep the temperature hot inside the *Alvin*.

The men sat close together in the small space on the ship, and they had only one light on – they needed to keep all their energy for their work at the bottom of the sea.

It was very strange and quiet sitting inside the *Alvin*, deep under the sea. It was lonely, and a little frightening, but the crew had a special telephone, and they used this to speak to the other people on the big ship above. They told them where they were, and what was happening. If they had any big problems, they could ask for help.

When it came near the sea bottom, the *Alvin* stopped, and the pilot switched on his big, powerful lights. The crew on the *Alvin* were excited now, and they looked out of the small windows of the ship. What could they see, so far below the surface?

The Alvin can stay under the water for up to 72 hours.

Going deeper …
In the deepest part of the sea, water pressure is 1,000 times more than the pressure at sea level. Normal submarines can't go this deep as the pressure would push the roof and floor together and make them flat.

… and deeper
In 1966, a submarine called *Trieste* made a new world record when it dived more than 11,000 metres.

How deep?
Alvin can dive deeper than a whale – but *Trieste* can go even deeper than this.

When they looked out of the windows, the crew saw huge, black rocks – they looked like tall buildings in the dark water. Near the small ship, they could see hot water vents – these are holes or cracks in the surface of the earth where hot water and smoke come out. The scientists were happy because they wanted to study what happens at these vents, where the hot water meets the cold water of the sea.

The hot water comes from volcanoes deep in the earth, and it comes out of the vents very fast. The temperature is extremely hot. The vents look very dangerous, but the scientists could see small plants and animals living near the hot water. They wanted to learn more about the lives of these amazing living things.

The pilot carefully took the *Alvin* nearer. Then one of the crew moved the big robot arm over and down to take a sample from the hot water. The scientists already knew something about this water, and that it would smell terrible, like bad eggs. Then the *Alvin* moved away and stopped on the floor of the ocean to get samples of other things.

After four hours, their work was finished. The pilot put down some heavy pieces of metal from a special part of the ship to make the *Alvin* lighter. Now they were ready to start their journey back up to the surface – the long journey would take about two hours. But the crew were happy. The scientists were excited about all the things they saw at the bottom of the ocean – it was an amazing trip.

Offshore Powerboats

What's that?
This strange-looking racing machine is called a swamp buggy. People race these machines through muddy swamps in Florida, USA. In the past, swamp buggies were used to hunt animals in the swamps.

Summer is the most important time for powerboat racers. Every year from June to November, powerboat teams from all over Europe and the Middle East meet together for a season of races. They race in the sea, off (away from) the shore. The teams are all very serious, and have spent a long time getting ready for the racing season. They all want the same thing – they are trying to win the offshore powerboat racing World Championships.

Offshore powerboats are huge, powerful machines. One powerboat weighs the same as five family cars, and it is about 13 metres long. They have been designed very carefully, and like many extreme machines, they are very expensive. The main body of the powerboat is a catamaran (two hulls joined together), and is made from special space-age materials – carbon fibre and Kevlar.

The special combination of carbon fibre and Kevlar is very light, but very, very strong. A light body helps the powerboat go faster, but the body must be strong, or it will break easily on the water. The inside of the powerboat is like the inside of a fighter plane: it is long and narrow, with the driver in front and another crew member sitting behind.

Safety is very important, and the two crew members have to wear seat belts, life jackets, and crash helmets. They also have an air supply. They can talk to each other, and to the other team members back on the shore, through special intercoms, like telephones, that are built into their crash helmets.

The intercom is one of the most important things for the crew. When the race begins, the engines are very noisy, and it is impossible to hear anyone talking. The two men on the powerboat have to talk together to control the machine. The crew on the shore can see what is happening and give advice.

Skirted boats
These are small hovercraft that can travel at 135 kph, just above the surface. They race every year at the World Championships in France, on a circuit over water and wet grass.

One or two?
In the past, offshore powerboats had only one body, and were open on top. Today, they have two bodies joined together and are closed on top. This makes them much safer.

Thin and fast
Cigarette boats are
very fast – they
have two powerful
engines and they
have won more
races than any
other boats. They
are called cigarette
boats because
people used them
to take cigarettes
illegally between
the Bahamas and
Florida, USA.

All the boats move around in the
water before the race begins, trying to get
the best starting position and trying not to
crash into one another! The race course is
marked out on the water with special floats,
called buoys. During the race, the boats have
to go round the buoys.

Inside each boat, the driver sits at the
front and checks the controls, ready to start the
race. The throttleman sits behind, and controls
the engines – he decides how much power they
need. He controls the propeller at the back of
the boat. He watches the wind and the waves
carefully, and this helps him to decide what
to do next.

One way to make a boat go faster is to drive into the wind. This lifts the front of the boat out of the water. However, the throttleman has to be very careful then. If the boat goes off the top of a wave and starts to fly through the air, he must cut the power quickly and slow the propeller down. If the propeller turns round too fast in the air, it can break!

The throttleman is always busy, changing the power from the engines and the speed of the propeller. When he does his job well, he can add an extra kilometre an hour to the speed of the boat. This can make all the difference between boats, and help win the race. But at speeds of 240 kph, the throttleman has to move quickly!

Slow down!
When the sea is rough, with a lot of waves, it can slow a powerboat down by 80 kph or more.

Jet boats
In New Zealand, people race small jet boats along shallow rivers. The boats have no propellers under them.

Formula 1 boats
These racing boats are fast and very powerful. Each boat has only one person inside, and has two parts (like offshore powerboats). They can go from 0 to 160 kph in five seconds.

Speed record
The *Spirit of Australia* was a hydroplane. In 1978, Ken Warby drove it and made a new world speed record on water, travelling at 514 kph.

Hydroplane Racing

Hydroplane racing is the fastest and most dangerous of all the water sports. On a racecourse of four kilometres, the best of these machines can travel down the straight parts of the course at a speed of 320 kph. They have to slow down at corners – but only a little! They can go round a corner at an amazing 250 kph. Because they are so fast and dangerous, many people think these hydroplane races are very exciting to watch.

Air in bottles
Hydroplane drivers carry enough oxygen for 45 minutes. They can use this if the boat turns over in the water.

The hydroplanes travel on the surface of the water, but they only touch the water a little. They travel on air between the boat and the water. But every time the boat touches the water, it makes a terrible noise. Because of the speed, the boat hits the water very hard, and the body shakes violently.

All this noise and movement makes life very difficult for the driver, and sometimes the boat shakes around so much that it is difficult for the driver to see anything. But the race lasts about twenty minutes, and the driver must stay in complete control – to go fast, he has to keep the boat as high out of the water as possible. At the same time, he has to get past the other boat if he wants to win the race. That may sound easy, like overtaking another car on the road, but in fact it is very difficult!

The rules say that when one boat goes past another, it can't go right in front of the other one until it is more than five boat lengths ahead. This is because a boat travelling fast throws up a mountain of water into the air behind it. If all this water comes down in front of another boat, the situation will be very dangerous. The water will fall in the path of the other boat, and push away the air it is travelling on. When this happens, the water pushes the second boat up into the air and it somersaults (turns over). It is an amazing thing to see.

Power crazy
A hydroplane is so powerful it can go at crazy speeds. Its engine is actually four times more powerful than the engine of a Formula 1 car.

No protection
In the past, hydroplanes were open on top, but there were more and more accidents as the boats got faster. Now the top is closed and the drivers sit inside, where it is safer.

A way out
Hydroplanes have two escape doors for the driver to use in emergencies. One door is at the front, and the other is under the boat. This is important if the boat turns over.

Speed king
Hydroplanes, like drag cars, can race over a 400-metre course. The *Spirit of Texas* set a 400-metre record of 5.5 seconds.

A hydroplane has a very clever design, which helps it to move through water very easily. It has two hulls (bodies) at the front, which are very light, but only one at the back. As the boat goes faster and faster, the two front hulls lift up into the air.

This means that the boat does not have to push the heavy water to the side, like other boats, as it travels along. It is much easier to travel through air. With only one hull at the back and a propeller in the water, there is the smallest possible contact with the water. This means that most of the power of the engine goes straight into the speed.

But hydroplanes have more than a clever design to make them go faster. These boats have a huge helicopter engine to give them their amazing power.

A team of top mechanics works on the engine to make it better and better – until it has an amazing 4,200 horsepower. But what does that mean? Well, it is enough power for forty-two normal family cars!

But speed like this also means danger for the people inside. In the past, hydroplaning has killed many drivers. When there was an accident, the drivers had nothing to protect them. Because of this, drivers today have more protection. They sit in the driver's seat, and there is a strong roof on top. They are closed in, but they have two escape doors to use in an emergency.

This has not stopped accidents happening during these races – it is still a very fast and dangerous sport. But today, if a driver is in an accident, he usually lives.

Strange fuel
Many hydroplane engines use alcohol, gas, or other strange mixtures of fuel. These give more power than the petrol or diesel we use in cars.

Next biggest
After the Mi-26, the next biggest helicopter is the Chinook. It can carry about one-third as much as the Mi-26.

Smallest of all
The world's smallest helicopter can only carry one person. In fact, the helicopter weighs about the same as a small adult.

Mi-26 Helicopter

The two big engines coughed and smoked when the world's biggest helicopter, Russia's Mi-26, started up. No-one nearby could hear anything because of the noise from the engines.

A few seconds later, the eight rotor blades on top of the helicopter started to turn round. As they moved through the air, they threw up the dust on the ground, making it difficult to see. The rotor blades got faster and faster, and soon you couldn't see the different blades – only a single disc. This disc was huge – it was wide enough to park ten lines of cars under it.

Finally, with another loud noise, the huge helicopter started to move, and slowly it lifted itself up into the air. The helicopter was answering an emergency call, and the pilot had a special job to do. He was on his way to the Ural Mountains in Russia, where there was a big problem – forest fires.

A number of fires were burning in the forest, and already huge areas were destroyed. Now the situation was getting worse. The fires were near the roads and villages, and people living in the area were in a lot of danger. The firefighters who were working in the area needed all the help they could get.

There are five people in the crew of an Mi-26, and they have to be able to move fast. This time they were ready and in the air only a few minutes after the emergency call came through. Their job was to take more firefighters into the area of the fires, and there was no time to wait around. Lives were in danger.

Power machines
The two engines on the Mi-26 are sixty times as powerful as a truck's engines.

That is why there were now 78 firefighters sitting close together inside the helicopter. Each person had a parachute and a special bag with firefighting equipment. They were ready to jump out of the helicopter at the right moment and to land near the fire. They knew they had a very difficult job in front of them, and that the other firefighters on the ground needed them as soon as possible.

Fuel tanks
The fuel tanks on the Mi-26 can hold enough fuel to take a family car halfway round the world. But they only take the Mi-26 480 kilometres.

60 years ago
In 1939, a Russian engineer called Sikorsky, living in the USA, built the first working helicopter with only one rotor.

1,500 years ago
The idea behind a helicopter is more than 1,500 years old. Then, the Chinese had a toy called a flying top. This toy used rotors made from feathers to fly.

Back and forward
A helicopter's rotor blades move in two directions, so a helicopter can fly forwards and backwards.

When they came near the fire, the crew on the helicopter could see where the danger was – a huge wall of smoke filled the air in front of them. They could not see through all the smoke, and it was difficult to know where to take the firefighters.

The pilot looked around, and then he saw a narrow road, a few kilometres west of the smoke. This was the place he was looking for, and he moved the huge helicopter nearer to the road.

But there was still a problem. The road was very narrow, and the helicopter couldn't land on it – it was too big. So the pilot kept the machine above the road while the crew opened the big doors at the back of the machine.

It was time to go. One by one, the firefighters jumped out of the helicopter. When they were clear of the back of the helicopter, they pulled the special cord to open their parachutes. Slowly they floated down towards the road and on to the grassy area beside it.

Ten minutes later, all of the 78 men were on the ground safely. They took off their parachutes and picked up their firefighting equipment. Soon they were beside the others, trying to stop the fires. Back on the helicopter, the crew closed the huge back doors again and got ready to fly away. The front of the helicopter went down in the air a little as it turned round, then flew back to get more help.

The X-15

Spacesuits
The pilots of the X-15 wore the same spacesuits as the astronauts who first flew into space.

How many?
Three X-15s flew a total of 199 times, over a period of nine years. The last flight of an X-15 was in 1968.

The huge B-52 bomber moved noisily down the runway and took off into the air. But this time it wasn't carrying any bombs – it had a small, black machine under its right wing. It didn't look like a machine, it looked more like a newspaper which it was carrying under its wing!

The "newspaper" was in fact an X-15, a very small, very powerful plane. This was a new experiment by the US Air Force. The Air Force wanted to check if it was possible to fly a plane, with someone inside, into space. The X-15 travelled like a passenger with the B-52 for the first part of the journey. This meant that the small X-15 only needed half the amount of fuel it would normally need, because a lot of fuel is used just getting a plane up into the air.

The small plane had no extra weight; it carried only one pilot and a lot of fuel. It wasn't really like a plane at all – it was more like a flying fuel tank! It had small, fat wings on its sides, and a rocket engine on its back.

The X-15 was the fifteenth special aircraft used by the Air Force for experiments like this.

They were designed to go fast and break records – the first of these aircraft was called the X-1. The scientists designed these planes to do experiments, and the first thing they wanted to do with these new X-15 planes was to go higher than thirty kilometres, and faster than three times the speed of sound. This seems amazing, but the X-15 did both of these things – and more. It was the first plane ever to fly into space, and it broke all the other records at the same time. It was now the highest, the fastest, and the most dangerous way to fly.

On the first trip, at the time arranged, the X-15 left its position under the wing of the B-52, and now it was flying alone. The pilot started the huge engine, and immediately the small plane flew straight up into the air. It looked like it was going to make a hole in the sky!

When it got to a height of sixty kilometres above the earth, there was very little air. There was no air to push against the wings.

X-1
The X-1 was the first plane to fly faster than the speed of sound.

Wrong engine
The X-15 couldn't use a jet engine like other planes because it was travelling into space. It used a rocket engine. A jet engine needs air to work, and there is no air in space.

The X-15 has no wheels at the back. It has special skids.

The pilot on the X-15 now used twelve very small rockets to change direction and steer. Up and up it went, climbing higher and higher in the sky. When all the fuel in the plane was finished, the X-15 was more than one hundred kilometres high. The pilot could look down and see the atmosphere below him, and the round shape of the earth's surface.

But was he in space? There is no exact line where the earth's atmosphere stops and space begins. Most space scientists agree that it happens about eighty kilometres up, so the pilot of the X-15 was officially outside the earth's atmosphere, and in space.

Because of this, the pilot and some of the team could now wear astronaut wings – a special badge that can only be worn by real astronauts. At the top part of its journey, the X-15 wasn't flying like an aeroplane, it was travelling like a spaceship and the crew were like astronauts.

Low fliers
Passenger jets fly about twelve kilometres high when they travel around the world. But compared with the X-15, this seems very low. The X-15 went nine times higher.

Now the X-15 was travelling along like a rocket at about 7,200 kph. That is just over six times the speed of sound. You can see how amazing this is when you compare it with a family car. At normal motorway speeds, a car would have to travel for three days and nights without stopping to go this far – and the X-15 could do it in one hour.

Now it was time to come back to earth. The pilot turned the plane a little and it started to glide (to fly without any engines or power). It was a very strange thing to see in the sky. The designers had had to make the plane as light as possible, so there were no wheels at the back of the plane. Instead of wheels there were two metal skids – these were lighter than normal wheels and they looked like two big skis.

The X-15 glided down nearer and nearer to the earth's surface, and when it landed, it skied along the ground until it stopped. It seemed like a long time, but the whole journey only took about ten minutes.

Getting hotter

At six times the speed of sound, the outside of the X-15 got very, very hot – an amazing 650°C. It needed a special metal surface to be able to take these high temperatures.

Getting bigger

Slower planes, like Concorde, also get very hot in a supersonic flight. Heat makes metal expand (get bigger), and Concorde's body "grows" by twenty centimetres in a supersonic flight.

Space Shuttle

The huge transport machine moved very slowly towards the launch pad. The machine was called the "Crawler" because it went so slowly – its fastest speed was just like a person walking. The Crawler was the largest transport machine in the world, and it was built to carry very heavy things. Now it was going at half speed because the thing it was carrying on top was huge and heavy.

On top of the Crawler was the space shuttle. This is the only plane that can take astronauts into space using its own power.

Earlier trips

Before the space shuttle, astronauts went into space in rockets. The huge Saturn V rockets were the largest and most powerful ones built.

Saturn V

Speed record

When it is in orbit around the earth, the space shuttle flies thirty times faster than a 747 jet. It would take ten minutes to fly from Los Angeles to New York.

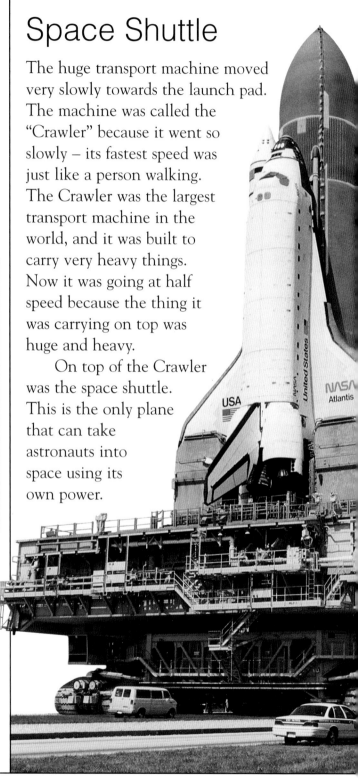

The main parts of the shuttle are the orbiter, the fuel tank, and the booster rockets. The crew of seven astronauts travel inside the orbiter. Under the orbiter there is a huge fuel tank to get the shuttle up through the earth's atmosphere. On the sides, there are two long, thin booster rockets to give the power for take-off. On this trip, the orbiter also carried a satellite to launch in space.

The Crawler arrived at the launch pad, and six hours later it was time for take-off. The countdown began ... 5, 4, 3, 2, 1, 0! With a huge roar and a blinding light, the shuttle moved up into the sky. Two minutes later, the booster rockets were empty and they fell away from the orbiter, back down to earth.

Now the main engines were switched on, and the fuel in the huge tank was used very quickly. The shuttle needed an enormous amount of fuel in a short time. When it was empty, the fuel tank fell away, and only the orbiter was left. It glided gently into its path, orbiting around the earth. The seven members of the crew were now 300 kilometres up.

Empty
When they are empty the two booster rockets fall back to earth. Then they are filled up and used on the next trip.

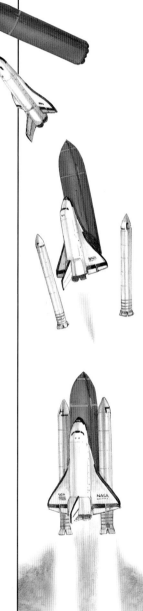

41

A long arm
The shuttle has a long robotic arm – as long as four cars parked one behind the other.

When they were in space, outside the earth's atmosphere, the seven astronauts in the crew and all their equipment were weightless. It was fun floating around, with nothing to hold them on the ground, but they had a lot of work to do.

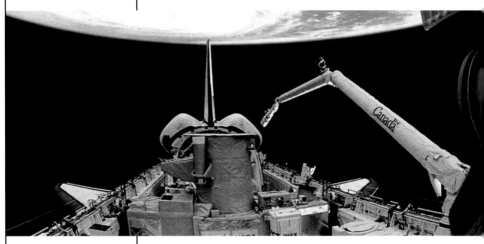

Space chair
Astronauts use a rocket-powered "armchair" to sit on when they work outside the shuttle.

Two of the astronauts got into their huge spacesuits, designed for working outside the shuttle. Then they went to the special room where the satellite was kept. One of the crewmen pushed a switch and the huge doors of the room opened. Then the astronauts used the shuttle's long, robotic arm to start to launch the satellite. They had to check everything very carefully, and it took a total of seven days to finish the checks and then launch the satellite.

After they launched the satellite and finished their work, it was time to return to earth. The astronauts sat in their seats and put on their special seat belts – they would need these when they got back into the earth's atmosphere. Then they heard the noise of the steering rockets, and the much louder noise of the main engine starting. The power from the main engine would take the shuttle out of orbit and back towards the earth.

When the orbiter hit the earth's atmosphere, it started to jump around, and dived down quickly – but the astronauts were all safely in their seats. The outside of the orbiter was bright red and on fire – this was the heat from moving through the air at thousands of kilometres an hour. The surface of the spaceship had a special cover to protect it and stop it from burning too much.

Now the orbiter didn't need its engines, and they were switched off. It came back to earth with no power – as a glider – and landed softly on the airport runway.

Space station
Several different countries are planning together to build and work in a space station in the earth's orbit. There will be a crew on the station all the time, showing that it is possible for humans to live in space.

Shuttle life
In space, the seven crew members on an orbiter live in the front part of the shuttle. All the equipment and the huge engines are in the back.

Ideas for the Future

No fuel tank
People who make new machines try to find ways to use less power. This solar-powered car runs on energy from the sun.

Speak to me
The Evoq has a special computer controlled by your voice. It helps the driver to travel safely.

Some ideas for machines for the future may sound very strange to us today. But pictures of the future always seem strange. One hundred years ago, nobody imagined the space shuttle – people then didn't have advanced technology, and could not see how space travel could be possible.

The Cadillac Evoq is an amazing sports car for the future. If you are ever inside one, don't look for the door handles, because there are none. The car opens by remote control.

This car can also "see" in the dark. Of course, all cars can "see" with their headlights at night but this car can see the area outside the lights. A special camera can pick up the body heat of people and animals quite far away. Their picture then appears on a special computer screen on the windscreen at the front of the car. The driver can see where they are, and he can steer the car safely away from danger.

The car can see anything behind it in the same way. It is like having eyes in the back of your head. So, the Evoq is a very clever design.

Another example of a machine for the future is the Flarecraft. On the water, the little Flarecraft L-325 is a boat that looks more like a plane. This kind of boat is called a wingship because it has two short, fat wings and a tail like an aeroplane. It also has a small propeller above the roof – like a helicopter. So the Flarecraft is a boat, plane, and helicopter in one design.

The Flarecraft is nine metres long, and it travels in a very special way. As it goes faster and faster in the water, it makes an area of high-pressure air under the wings. This pressure is strong enough to lift the wingship and its five passengers up into the air. Then it can travel along at speeds of up to 120 kph. It is a lot faster than a normal boat because it is easier to move through air than through water (moving through the heavy water pulls a boat back and uses more power). But it can't lift up very far – no more than the height of an adult.

Because of this, the wingship is still a boat and not an aeroplane. It can never really fly away. If it tries to fly any higher, the air pressure under the wings falls, and the wingship falls down onto the water again.

Flying on water
As the Flarecraft goes faster, it lifts up out of the water. At 80 kph, it takes off and flies just above the surface.

What's that?
This is a design for a new car called the Slug. It looks very strange.

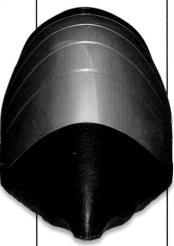

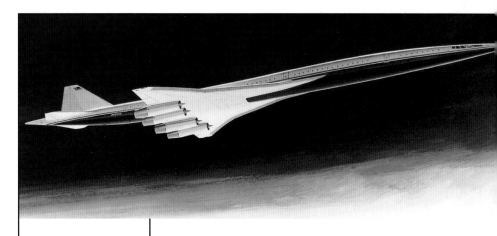

Speed machines
Supersonic planes in the future will be more than twice as long as Concorde!

Space rescue
The picture below shows an idea for a rescue ship in space. It would be like an ambulance, and would take people from the international space station back to a hospital on earth.

There are also some exciting plans for passenger planes in the future, and these may change the whole experience of air travel. Scientists and designers are working on a huge 300-seat jet aeroplane that will fly at a speed of 2,400 kph. That is more than twice the speed of sound! The plane will be able to travel from the USA to Japan in four hours. At the moment, the journey between these two countries takes about eight hours.

The aeroplane will travel faster than a bullet from a gun. When it is moving so fast, its nose at the front, and the ends of its wings at the sides, will become very hot – hot enough to bake a cake! This is a problem for the designers, and they have to use special metals on the outside (like the space shuttle). They need to use metals that can change from very hot to cold all the time without getting weaker. If a metal gets weak, it can crack or break and the plane will crash. Scientists in many countries are working hard to find new metals, or mixtures of metals, for these new aeroplane designs.

There is another problem for the scientists and designers. An aeroplane that goes fast enough to break the sound barrier (in other words a supersonic aeroplane) must have a long, pointed nose. But it is difficult for the pilots to see past this nose when they land or take off at the airport. The designers of Concorde found one answer to this problem – they built a nose that can move up and down when the pilot wants to see more clearly. The new plane has a different answer – it will have no windows at the front at all! Instead of looking out of the window, the pilot will use a computer screen to see what is in front of the plane.

There are many possible, amazing machines for the future. Here is one strange design for a space transporter in the future. It is designed to carry people and equipment in and out of space like the space shuttle today.

What about you – what do you think extreme machines will look like in the future?

Space travel
Many people dream about space travel, and there are some amazing plans for different spaceships. Here is an idea for a space transporter.

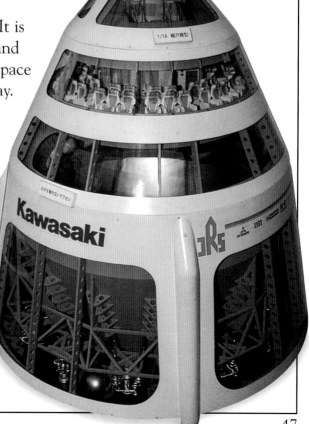

47

Glossary

aerodynamic
Something that is
designed to move
easily through the air.

Alvin
The name of a deep-
sea submersible.

Black Rock Desert
A long, flat piece of
very dry land in
Nevada, USA.

booster rocket
A smaller rocket used
on a spaceship to give
extra power, e.g. on
take-off.

buoy
Something that floats
on top of the water as
a mark or guide.

catamaran
A boat with two
separate bodies (hulls)
joined together.

crane
A machine for lifting
heavy things.

Crawler
A huge transporter
that is strong enough
to carry the space
shuttle.

drag car racing
Two cars race from
stop position to the
finish line in less than
10 seconds.

Evoq
A car of the future. It
is computerised and
can "see" in the dark.

Flarecraft L-325
A small boat (or
wingship) that flies
just above the water.

glide
To fly without any
engine power.

hydroplane racing
The fastest water
sport, where only the
back of the boat sits
in the water.

launch pad
The place where a
rocket or spaceship
takes off.

Le Mans
A town in France that
has one of the most
famous car races every
year.

Mi-26
The biggest helicopter
in the world.

orbiter
The part of the space
shuttle that carries
the astronauts and the
equipment.

pit
The place where
racing drivers stop
their cars to get petrol
and new tyres.

propeller
The part of a boat or
helicopter engine
(also called rotor)
that turns round.

submersible
A ship that can travel
deep under the sea.

throttleman
The person who
controls the
accelerator (engine
power).

Thrust SSC
The fastest car in the
world (1997), a car
that can travel at
supersonic speed.

treads
The deep lines on a
tyre (tyres with no
treads are called
slicks).

vent
An opening or hole in
the surface that air
can get through
(e.g. hot air vent).

world record
The best in the world
in one thing (the
fastest, highest,
deepest, etc.). When
you become the best
you break the old
world record.

X-15
The first aeroplane to
fly into space.